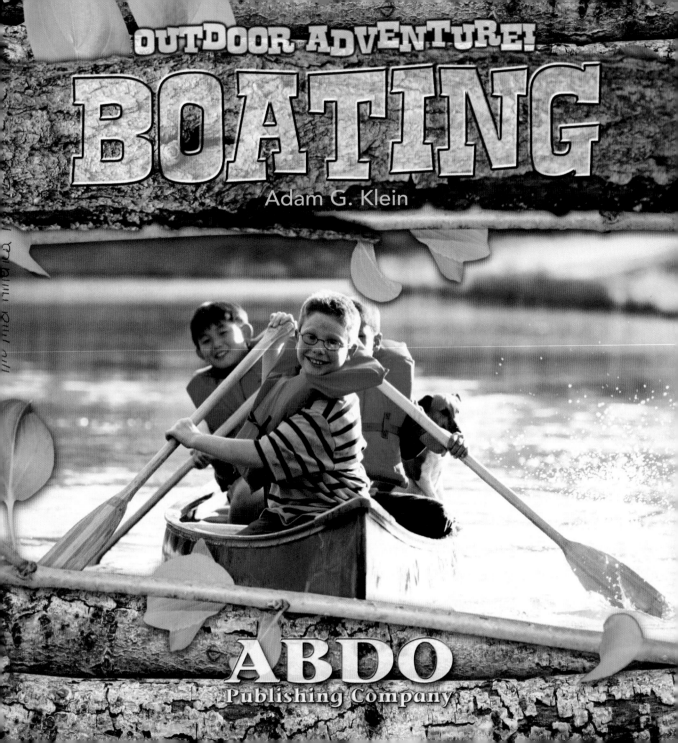

OUTDOOR ADVENTURE!
BOATING

Adam G. Klein

ABDO
Publishing Company

visit us at
www.abdopublishing.com

Published by ABDO Publishing Company, 8000 West 78th Street, Edina, Minnesota 55439.
Copyright © 2008 by Abdo Consulting Group, Inc. International copyrights reserved in all
countries. No part of this book may be reproduced in any form without written permission from the
publisher. The Checkerboard Library™ is a trademark and logo of ABDO Publishing Company.

Printed in the United States.

Cover Photo: Corbis
Interior Photos: Alamy p. 27; AP Images p. 17; Corbis pp. 1, 5, 15, 28, 29; Getty Images pp. 19, 23;
    iStockphoto pp. 7, 9, 10, 11, 12, 21, 26; Peter Arnold p. 25; U.S. Coast Guard p. 13

Series Coordinator: Rochelle Baltzer
Editors: Rochelle Baltzer, Megan M. Gunderson
Art Direction & Cover Design: Neil Klinepier

Library of Congress Cataloging-in-Publication Data

Klein, Adam G., 1976-
  Boating / Adam G. Klein.
      p. cm. -- (Outdoor adventure!)
  Includes index.
  ISBN 978-1-59928-956-4
  1. Boats and boating--Juvenile literature. I. Title.

GV775.3.K54 2008
797.1--dc22

                          2007029164

CONTENTS

A DAY AT SEA

"I thought you knew how to sail!" Jen yelled, panicking as water flooded into the tiny sailboat. Jason opened his mouth to apologize, but Jen quickly cut him off. "I mean, we're in the water! Should we be in the water?"

Jen clung to the side of the **capsizing** boat as Jason grabbed a rope. Jason placed his feet on the floor of the boat and leaned back with all his force. The sail reluctantly rose from the water, and the boat lifted upright. The sail snapped tight in the wind, shaking off water from the fall.

Suddenly, Jen felt silly about her earlier complaints. "Well, all right then," she said. Jason's amused look urged her to continue. "Thanks for taking me out today. It's really beautiful out here," she added. Jason smiled as he began to **bail** out the boat. Jen grinned and grabbed a pail to help.

The pastime of boating for pleasure is more than 300 years old. That's far older than baseball, golf, tennis, and almost any other outdoor sport!

ALL ABOARD

Worldwide, people enjoy boating for many reasons. Boats can take us places that we cannot reach by car or foot. Boating also benefits a person's health. Being in fresh air and on open water is energizing. There are many activities that can be done from a boat for exercise, too.

Some people fish from boats. Others use them for water sports, such as waterskiing or scuba diving. Still others use canoes, sailboats, or motorboats for racing. Each race has its own rules. But, boat owners are allowed to modify their boats for the best results. Some people race to win. Others might race just for fun!

Entertaining on a boat is enjoyable, too. Large watercraft can carry many people around a lake, down a river, or across an ocean.

A boat that is meant for long vacations has large sleeping cabins, a kitchen, a bathroom, and other necessities. Whether you prefer adventure or relaxation, boating could be the perfect choice!

TIP *Large boats should have a skipper. This person acts as a leader. He or she shows the crew how to use vital equipment, such as life jackets and fire extinguishers.*

Each year, there are about 78 million boaters and nearly 13 million registered boats operating on U.S. waterways.

BOW TO STERN

Boating is a long-standing tradition with many different terms. So, it is helpful to know some basic boating terms before setting off. The front of a boat is called the bow, and the back of a boat is named the stern. When facing the bow, the port side is to the left. The starboard side is to the right.

The body of a boat is called the hull. Hulls are made of steel, wood, or **fiberglass**. The two main hull types are displacement hulls and planing hulls. Displacement hulls push through water, while planing hulls ride on top of water. Hulls are designed in various shapes, too. The most common hull designs are round, flat, or V-shaped.

Round hulls are generally considered displacement hulls. They move easily at slow speeds. Planing hulls include flat hulls and some V-shaped hulls. Flat hulls reach high speeds but can be unstable in rough waves. So, some planing hulls have a V shape to offer a smoother ride.

Some boats have more than one hull. Additional hulls widen boats, making them less likely to **capsize**. Boats with two hulls are called catamarans. Three-hulled boats are named trimarans. Both boat types can ride fast and remain stable. So, they are often used for sports and recreation.

Modern catamarans were originally designed to resemble a type of Indonesian raft with two logs connected by planks. These rafts were up to 70 feet (21 m) long! Today's average catamaran is 40 feet (12 m) long.

TO FLOAT OR SINK

Do you know how boats float? Let's find out by conducting a simple experiment. Gather two equally sized pieces of tinfoil. Shape one piece into a boat and the other into a ball. Then, place both pieces in water. Why does one sink and the other float?

To understand, let's first learn about displacement. When an object is put in water it displaces, or pushes away, water. The volume of the displaced water is equal to the volume of the portion of the object that is underwater.

A boat lowers into water until the weight of the displaced water is equal to the boat's weight. A boat will only float if it is less dense than the water it sits in. In other words, a boat floats when it has a smaller mass per unit volume than the water. If a boat is carrying too much weight for its shape and size, it will sink.

So, why did the foil ball sink and the boat float? The ball's shape made it more dense than the water. And, the boat's shape made it less dense than the water. The density of salt water and freshwater varies, too. Salt water is denser than freshwater. That's why it's easier to float in an ocean than in a lake!

A flat hull displaces very little water while moving. Flat-bottom boats are stable in calm waters. They are ideal for hunting or fishing in narrow areas, such as rivers.

Deep V-shaped boats move slowly because they displace a lot of water. However, V-bottom boats offer a smooth ride in rough waters.

Many canoes and sailboats have round hulls. Round-hull boats are typically easier to maneuver at slow speeds than flat-bottom boats.

POWER BY MOTOR

Motorboats are a great way to travel. They are easy to use, which makes them ideal for carefree days on the water. Motorboats are made in many sizes. They range in length from 8 to 100 feet (2 to 30 m) or longer. Popular types of motorboats include waterskiing boats, fishing boats, and day-cruising boats.

There are different ways to move a motorboat. A **propeller** is the most common method. The engine that powers a propeller can be inboard or outboard. An inboard engine sits inside the hull and is ideal for large, fast boats.

An outboard engine lays outside

An outboard motor attaches to a stern or sits in a well within the hull.

Most motorboats have space for up to six passengers.

the hull and is attached to the stern. These motors are lighter, smaller, and more affordable than inboard motors.

Another way of moving a motorboat is by jet. In the early 1950s, Sir William Hamilton of New Zealand developed the marine jet engine.

This type of engine is powered by internal **combustion**. The engine shoots out water, which drives the craft forward. Jet boaters can drive through shallow waters. That is because they don't have to worry about the spinning blades of a **propeller** hitting rocks or other objects.

ROWING A BOAT

Motorboats are fun, but other kinds of boats provide different experiences. Canoes and kayaks (KEYE-aks) can reach places that motorboats cannot. They can drift through shallow waters where motorboats would hit ground.

Because they are not operated by motor, canoes and kayaks are **environmentally** friendly. Boaters use their own strength to paddle them. For this reason, they are allowed in places where water must remain pure.

Most canoes can hold two or three passengers. Usually, one paddler sits at each end of a canoe. A third person sits in the middle. Canoes are easy to transport. They can be strapped on top of cars. Canoes can also be portaged, or carried, using rope **toggles** that are attached to both ends.

Canoes are often used for camping because they offer plenty of storage space. Some campers pack their equipment inside a canoe and paddle everything to a campsite. This method works best when camping along a chain of lakes or rivers.

TIP *When loading your canoe, make sure to evenly distribute the weight. This maintains balance so that the canoe remains level in the water.*

Kayaks carry only one or two people. These shallow, rather flat-bottomed boats move fast and can easily tip over. But tipping over in a kayak is actually fun! Kayakers shift their body weight and use a double-bladed paddle to turn upright.

The two types of kayaks are flatwater and whitewater. Flatwater kayaks are used to paddle on calm rivers, lakes, and seacoast waters. Whitewater kayaks are used on river rapids.

BY WAY OF WIND

In 4500 BC, sailing ships were made in **Mesopotamia**. Since then, people around the world have enjoyed sailing. From an 8-foot (2-m) **dinghy** (DIHNG-ee) to a 400-foot (122-m) **yacht** (YAHT), sailing is a grand time! With practice, anyone can learn to sail.

Sailors **manipulate** the force of wind to move their sailboats. A large and small sail must catch wind to move a sailboat. Larger sailboats have more sails. Sailors must pay close attention to the direction and strength of the wind. If they are not alert, a strong wind can quickly heel, or tip, their boat.

For stability, a sailboat has a long extension called a keel on the bottom of its hull. There are various types of keels. Most of them are made from timber, metal, or other strong materials.

Without a keel, a sailboat would probably heel. If a boat heels, sailors quickly take action to upright it. They have to make sure the boat does not **capsize**.

AMERICA'S CUP

The America's Cup is an international sailboat racing competition. A yacht from a defending country competes against a yacht from a challenging country. The competing yachts are determined in separate series of elimination rounds. The winning yacht receives the America's Cup. This coveted cup is the oldest trophy in international sports.

The America's Cup is named after *America*. In 1851, this American boat defeated boats from England's most prestigious yacht club. *America*'s owners received a trophy called the Squadron Cup. In 1857, they gave the cup to the New York Yacht Club to use in international competitions. Soon, it became known as the America's Cup.

America's Cup Highlights

- *There had already been nine contests for the America's Cup before the first modern Olympic Games were held in 1896!*

- Reliance, *winner of the 1903 cup, was the world's largest single-masted sailboat until 1998. It stretched 143 feet (44 m) from bow to stern.*

- Australia II *became the first challenger ever to win the cup when it defeated* Liberty *in 1983. That year, the United States gave up the trophy for the first time.*

SAFETY AT SEA

Before setting out, it is important for boaters to become familiar with boating safety. First, they should always tell someone on land where they are going and when they expect to return.

To prevent onboard accidents, boaters must obey a boat's capacity limit. This limit refers to the amount of persons or weight that a boat can safely carry.

There are also certain items that should always be onboard. Each passenger should wear a personal flotation device (PFD) at all times. If passengers fall into the water, PFDs will save their lives. PFDs are classified by number. The lower the number, the better the PFD floats.

Boats should contain a first aid kit, too. A basic kit includes a first aid manual, rubbing alcohol, bandages, tweezers, and plastic gloves. Certain boats are also required to carry visual signals, such as flares, in case of an emergency.

Boaters should wear sunscreen with an **SPF** of at least 15, as well as sunglasses. They should also bring high-energy foods and plenty of water, especially on hot days.

At night or during poor visibility, boaters must attach lights to their boats so others can see them. A red light signals the port side of a boat, and a green light signals the starboard side. A white light indicates a boat's stern. Larger boats or ships use other lights.

To make sure that your PFD fits securely, test it out! In the water, it should not raise above your chin.

COMMUNICATION

A cellular telephone is a good way to communicate from a boat, but there are limitations. During an emergency, you would need to know the phone number of someone on a nearby boat. For this reason, it is better to have a way to talk to anyone nearby.

Therefore, boats are often equipped with very high frequency (VHF) radios. VHF radios effectively transmit messages to boats within 20 to 25 miles (32 to 40 km).

Boaters also use air horns to communicate. They honk them in long and short bursts. Each pattern of bursts has a different meaning. One short burst means a boat intends to pass another boat on its port side. Five short bursts in response to a passing signal means danger. Boaters can use horn patterns to convey many things.

Lighthouses are another helpful boating aid. These tall structures send out light signals to help boaters navigate. From the sea, a lighthouse can be identified by its shape or by the color or flash pattern of its light. Lighthouses guide

At one time, lighthouses were operated by lighthouse keepers who lived in or near the lighthouse. Today, lighthouses are automated, so they do not need keepers.

boaters to their **destinations** and help them establish their positions at sea.

OBEY THE RULES

Understanding boating traditions, following rules, and observing onboard **etiquette** is important. This shows respect to other boaters and to the sport itself. Respectful boaters give other boaters privacy, yet they remain ready to assist if necessary.

Ports, channels, and rivers are often crowded with boats. When passing, boaters slow down as much as possible and pass port side to port side. Barges and sailboats are difficult to **maneuver** (muh-NOO-vuhr), so boaters passing these craft give them extra space. Boaters also give fishing boats plenty of room so that fish aren't scared away.

In certain areas, differently colored markers called buoys (BOO-eez) float in water to indicate different things. For example, red and green buoys help center a boat that is headed upstream or into a port. Boaters keep red buoys to the right of their boat and green buoys to the left. Buoys also have numbers on them that help boaters navigate.

Boaters use numbered buoys to find their location on a map. Red buoys are even-numbered and green buoys are odd-numbered.

ANCHORS AWEIGH

Boaters use various types of anchors to hold boats in place in the water. Some anchors are ideal for small boats, and others are designed to hold larger craft. Sometimes, the type of ground also makes a difference when choosing an appropriate anchor.

The traditional fisherman's anchor holds well on rocky bottoms. It has two curved hooks that catch on rocks to secure a boat. Danforth anchors work best on sandy or muddy grounds. The end of this anchor is a flat wedge that swivels into sand or mud. Plow anchors resemble a farmer's plow and dig into weed-covered bottoms.

When securing an anchor, a boater makes sure to leave extra slack in the rope. This allows the boat to freely move up and down with the waves. Otherwise, this movement can **dislodge** the anchor.

When anchoring, boaters consider tides. A boat can get damaged or lost if a person does not plan for a tide change. When the boat is ready to move again, the anchor is lifted.

In most places, the tide changes only a few feet. In Canada, the Bay of Fundy has the highest tides in the world. There, the water can rise and fall as much as 50 feet (15 m) each day! The Bay of Fundy looks much different at low tide (above left) and at high tide (above right).

SUN AND STORMS

A bright, sunny sky can become dark and cloudy with little notice. Boaters must pay attention to signs in the sky, such as cloud patterns. Isolated, high clouds indicate good weather. But dark, crowding clouds are signs of worsening weather.

Boaters can also watch the direction and speed of wind to determine the approaching weather. Wind speed is measured in knots. One knot is equal to 1.15 miles per hour (1.85 km/h). Winds of 7 to 10 knots (13 to 19 km/h) are considered a gentle breeze. Winds from a violent storm gust at 56 to 63 knots (104 to 117 km/h).

Some boaters use barometers to predict weather. Barometers measure air pressure. Changes in air pressure indicate changes in weather.

Sometimes it is difficult to **predict** weather. So, boaters use radios to listen to weather updates. Most weather reports are from land. Boaters must remember that wind moves much faster over open water. If the wind becomes too strong, boaters need to wait out the weather. When the sun comes out, boaters can enjoy the water again!

Boaters should stay aware of weather conditions to avoid danger.

BOAT UPKEEP

Maintaining a boat is satisfying for many people. The type of maintenance required depends on a boat's construction. For example, wooden boats need different upkeep than boats made from **fiberglass**.

Usually, boat owners complete a thorough inspection at the end of the boating season. They take pride in making sure engines are tuned up, ropes are not **frayed**, and sails are not torn. They also check safety equipment. Fire extinguishers, flares, PFDs, and first aid kits must be inspected at least once every year.

In addition, boat owners should look for scratches and rotten areas on their boats. Small, hidden areas of rotten wood can grow into huge

Even small amounts of cleaning products can harm underwater creatures. So, it is best to use environmentally friendly products and to clean a boat on land.

holes if untreated. Owners can use their boats longer if they keep everything in shape. This way, they may enjoy many more adventures! As long as boaters follow safety rules, most outings are good experiences. Even though Jason and Jen had a minor mishap, they teamed up to enjoy smooth sailing for the rest of the day. So, get out there and have fun on your own boating journeys!

Boating can be a relaxing outing with family and friends. Activities such as sailing, paddling, and waterskiing are good exercise, too!

GLOSSARY

bail - to clear water from a boat by throwing it over a side.

capsize - to turn over.

combustion - the act or instance of burning.

destination - the place someone or something is going to.

dinghy - a small sailboat.

dislodge - to force out of a secure or settled position.

environment - all the surroundings that affect the growth and well-being of a living thing.

etiquette - good manners or polite behavior accepted by a society.

fiberglass - glass in fibrous form used for making various products.

frayed - raveled or worn out.

maneuver - to make changes in direction and position for a specific purpose.

manipulate - to treat or operate in a skillful way.

Mesopotamia - an ancient region in which the world's earliest civilization developed. It included the area that is now eastern Syria, southeastern Turkey, and most of Iraq.

predict - to declare in advance.

propeller - a device that has a revolving central part with blades. The spinning blades move a vehicle, such as a boat or an airplane.

SPF - sun protection factor. A classification of the U.S. Food and Drug Administration of the degree to which a sunblock or a sunscreen will protect the skin from sunburn.

toggle - a pin, a bolt, or a rod put through a loop in a rope to serve as a hold for the fingers.

yacht - a sailboat used for racing or a large, usually motor-driven, boat used for pleasure cruising.

WEB SITES

To learn more about boating, visit ABDO Publishing Company on the World Wide Web at www.abdopublishing.com. Web sites about boating are featured on our Book Links page. These links are routinely monitored and updated to provide the most current information available.

INDEX